Moments In Time
Volume One

Poetry, Prose and Photography
By
Catherine MLP Pagano

~

D1441359

Published in the United States of America
ISBN-13: 978-1530555048
ISBN-10: 1530555043

~

www.cmlppart-photography.blogspot.com

Carol, It's been such a blast working through you through photo groups & photo shots & photo groups to many! Looking forward to many more fun years! Catherine MLP Pagano

This book is dedicated to my mother; a lovely, creative, talented lady in her own right; who has weathered a lifetime of her own challenges and still has the grace to find some humor in it all.
I love you.

Special acknowledgements go out to Geert, for showing by example, that self-publishing is a real possibility for me. Glenda and Lily; without your kind words and encouragement to publish my poems, I never would have gone down this path. And to everyone, everywhere, who touched my life at any given moment in time, in both positive and negative ways; you have been the inspiration for my poetry and prose. And last but certainly not least, the membership of my photo challenge group; you have stuck with me, for many years, on my photographic journey of always striving to improve, compose and create beautiful photography. Your comradery and enthusiasm keeps pushing me to reach higher and learn more! This book is a step in that direction. Thank you all!

It's All Art

I am the poet, the musician, the dancer, the artist.

I create music with words, I create motion with paints,

I create words with dance.

All the arts are interconnected.

All arts are the means to create

And bring ideas and visions to reality.

All artists have an inner need

To be seen and to be heard,

Through their chosen medium.

Sometimes they struggle to release these ideas,

Sometimes it seems impossible

For others to understand what they are trying to say.

Yet through it all they persist.

They have a deep seeded need to get their message

conveyed.

They bare their souls in this pursuit.

Some of their creations are obvious,

Others only hint at a meaning.

Some bring laughter or tears,

Others bring reflections or convey futures untold.

This is my pen, my brush, my bow,

It's just an extension of my soul.

I move my body with the rhythm of the Earth;

I allow these inner feelings to pour out and give birth...

To Art.

Dance

Dance to the beat of nature,

Move to the rhythm of the wind,

Listen to the whispers of silence,

Reach for the peace within.

Ever Have One Of Those Days?

Now that I have a quiet moment
I can reflect back on the hours of this day
None were too short
None were too long
The hours...well
They just passed away.
One by one,
All in the proper order of things
The day was gone too soon.
I grasp for a moment,
To find a time when my mind was
challenged.
I try to think of anything memorable.
But in the course of this day,
Sigh,
The only thought I remember thinking
was...
When can I get away?

The Tale of Mr. Bear and Miss Squirrel

Mr. Bear was unaware that Miss Squirrel wanted ALL of his attention.

He thought it was cute how she never stayed mute;
And always would tell him he's funny.

She followed him one day and saw a little bird fly away.

She questioned what he was doing?

He smiled and said "I'm so lucky to have a little bird friend!"

She only saw red and told him "that friendship must end".

He told her "no way; now please go away and leave me alone".

She mumbled and grumbled and her heart turned to stone.

Miss Squirrel knew she could not catch the little bird.

The little bird lived too far away.

But in her mind she plotted and planned to get her revenge one day.

On a cool October day, Mr. Bear was unaware

That Miss Squirrel planned his demise.

She snuck up behind him...oh my, oh misery, what was she doing?

She was tying a noose; while from her mouth harsh words were spewing.

Before either one knew it, the deadly deed had been done.

Miss Squirrel puffed her chest and exclaimed "I have won!"

Then slowly she realized and questioned what she had done.

"Yesterday I had a friend and today I have none!"

"Oh no" she cried; "I must revive him".

But try as she may, try as she might,

Mr. Bear was gone...there was no more light.

Astral Projection

When the sun is shining bright
The world is open to my sight,
But when the darkness fills the sky,
I spread my wings and start to fly.
My soul is in flight
As it soars through the night.
I fly over mountains and across the sea,
I fly over rivers and valleys and trees.
I feel no heat, I feel no cold.
I only feel freedom for adventures untold.
I dance in the sky and twirl in the air,
Nothing holds me back when I'm flying up
there.
The elation I feel is beyond explanation,
It's an overwhelming sense of total
gratification.
And then for a moment a bright light
pierces my eyes;
Damn, it's time to wake up, it's time to
rise.
I carry that gratifying feeling with me
Throughout the long day;
For I know that night is coming
And again I'll soar away.

Go Ahead, Smile

I have a song in my heart,
A song I would like to share.
It's a song of peace, a song of love,
A song that says I care.
I know that you do not know me,
But really that's okay.
I care about you anyways
And wish you a wonderful day.
Now wouldn't it be nice
If everyone felt this way?
Don't waste your time on grumpiness,
Get out there and smile today.
Smile for the sunshine, smile for the rain,
Smile for the simple things that bring no pain.
Smile for the moment, smile for the entire day;
Smile at your fellow man, even if he just walks away.
I have a song in my heart,
I wish I had a voice to sing;
It's a song that wishes everyone
The best of everything.

AWAKE

While I'm awake
And my eyes are open wide,
I don't want to waste
A minute of living,
Or bury my head and hide.
I welcome the sun,
I embrace the light;
I'm thankful every day,
For such a beautiful sight.

Friendship

The path leading to the key of friendship
Can be riddled with thorns and flowers.
Shall we take a stroll?
I'll meet you at the entrance,
Together we'll enter the maze.
We'll learn about each other
And share a thought or two.
Shall we bring a lunch?
We will laugh and cry, be happy and sad;
Respect each other's differences
And welcome the time spent together.
Shall we play hide and seek?
We will take comfort in the companionship
And look forward to epic debates;
Find humor in our faults with gracious modesty
And discover hidden talents we never knew we had.
Shall we sit quietly for a while?
We don't always have to talk a lot
And we don't always have to agree;
It's just nice to know that we share a common bond
And are both thankful for these moments in time.
Shall we call it a day?
Yes, a friendship can be a valuable and precious commodity.
It's not often we can call someone a friend of our own.
Rarely does someone come along and fit right in with your life; even
when they are far away, it's just nice to know they care.
Shall we meet again?

All Is Not What It Appears To Be

A Warning To Myself

Somewhere out there is a soul who is waiting...
Waiting for me to say hello.
Somewhere out there is a soul who is waiting...
Waiting for me to look their way.
Somewhere out there is a soul who is waiting...
Waiting for me to acknowledge them.
Somewhere out there is a soul who is waiting...
Waiting for me to reach out to them.
Somewhere out there is a soul who is waiting...
Waiting for me to open my eyes.
Somewhere out there is a soul who is waiting...
Waiting for me to open my heart.
Somewhere out there is a soul who is waiting...
Waiting for me to embrace them.
Somewhere out there is a soul who is waiting...
Waiting for me to understand them.
Somewhere out there is a soul who is waiting...
Waiting for me to accept them.
Somewhere out there is a soul who is waiting...
Waiting for me.
But right now,
I am just too blind to see.

The Hunter and the Fox

I can sense his presence,
There's vibration in the air.
I can smell his human odor,
He's searching for my lair.
I shall sit here as if I'm frozen,
Not a motion will I make.
I'll watch his every movement,
My safety is at stake.
He bends down low and he looks around,
He walks in circles as he studies the ground.
What is he looking for, what does he see?
Is he lost in my wilderness or is he hunting me?
He fiddles with a box and attaches it to a tree.
Is this some kind of trap?
Perhaps I should run and flee.
But wait just a minute, he's starting to walk away.
I smell no food for bait, sniff, sniff...
Guess I'm safe for another day.
As I watch the hunter leave,
I note the direction that he goes.
I can always follow him; his smell will lead my nose.
But first I must do something; an action without fail...
To mark his box as mine: I lift my leg and then my tail.

The Silent Goodbye

Without a word, in the blink of an eye,
My friend had vanished, without saying goodbye.
It's hard to know what was on my friend's mind,
To vacate without a word is just so unkind.
In this cyber age it is easy to lose sight,
That a friend is not a "friend";
It's just another word to write.
No matter what your reasons for this silence that I hear,
I wish you only happiness, good health and good cheer.
So here I'll sign off with a frown and a sigh...
And wish my silent friend,
A friendly goodbye.

My Inner Lifeline

There's a place that I go
When I'm feeling down;
It's a sanctuary of sorts,
It's void of any sound.
I can step inside this space
And know that I'll be okay.
I can unburden my thoughts
And prepare for another day.
This chamber, it is hidden,
Within the recesses of my mind.
It allows me to balance out,
When people are so unkind.
Here I can refresh myself
With encouragement from older souls;
They remind me that I have worth
And I can achieve many more goals.
I must never depend
On people from the outside.
To find inner peace;
Just trust my inner guide.
The process takes only a moment,
When defined by current time
But the effects are everlasting;
This space is my soul's lifeline.

My Wall

This wall is mine
I've built it one stone at a time.
Every stone has a story
From a moment in my life.
Some represent happy times,
Some reflect strife.
Some times were good,
Some times were bad;
But each and every stone
Is a memory that I have.
I build this wall
With careful deliberation,
I want it to withstand
Life's many conflagrations.
It's a tapestry of my life,
Easy for anyone to see;
Because each and every stone
Harbors a little part of me.

Whispering Into The Wind

If I whisper into the wind

Who in the world will hear?

Can words be carried around the globe?

Can the words alone be clear?

I had a vision that this would work

So I'll step outside and try...

I hope you get my message;

On the wind my words will fly.

A Better Way

The world is full of beauty
And yet, the world is full of strife.
I can't help but wonder
About this complicated life.
For every good thing that happens,
There is an equal measure of bad.
I get that this keeps things in balance,
But I'd rather be happy than sad.
Sometimes we reach out to that friendly voice we hear
Only to find out that their motives were unclear.
And even though our judgement was certainly flawed
Not everyone is bad, there's so many to applaud.
So the best we can do is continue on our way.
Make it a point to make it a better day.
Seek out beauty, whether grand or small
Then capture those moments and share them all.
Then maybe, eventually
We will surprisingly find...
That all that is bad is not equally blind.

Liquid Diamonds

Liquid diamonds
Pour from your eyes.
Your heart has been broken,
This I realize.
No comfort, no warmth,
No wisdom, no gain,
Comes from the deluge
Of grief's holy rain.
Only time can stop the tears
If you will it to be so.
You've got to work through your sorrow
And don't allow it to grow.
A word of caution
I must interject here;
For the sake of all others
Who hold you so dear;
You must not stay
In your grief too long,
Or you'll stop hearing
Your own life's song.
I would like to buffer your sorrow,
I would gladly shoulder your pain,
But acceptance is something
You alone must attain.

Oh Those Challenges

Everyone faces challenges;
Some are planned and some are not,
Some are surprises that bring laughter and joy,
Some create havoc, with the intent to destroy.
You must look for the good, embrace all that is well,
For the challenges you face
Only time will tell.
Have you ever had a challenge,
That is like a painful pebble in your shoe?
Well shake out that pebble,
Reclaim your shoe.
Be glad it wasn't a boulder
That rolled over you!
Embrace that pain,
Take it in stride,
Life's full of challenges,
There's nowhere to hide.
One day you'll look back,
With a shake of your head;
"What the hell was I thinking?
It's not like I'm dead!"
I guess what I'm trying to say,
In the most unsubtle way...you are only human.
And even though pain sometimes comes your way,
Remember that the dust of tomorrow,
Was just the pebbles of today.

People Of The Mist

The fog rolls in, it blankets the ground.
It's so thick I can barely see my hand.
Reaching into the fog I imagine touching the souls
That have floated in with the white mist.
I blink my eyes quickly, what did I just see?
Is this misty field the convergence of two realms?
If I just stand here will they pass me by? Can they see me?
Should I speak or can they hear my thoughts?
All of a sudden I feel a cool whisper of wind touch my neck.
Another feathery touch slides down my arm.
What a strange sensation this fog brings on.
What just brushed against my leg?
It was soft and light, hardly a touch at all.
I close my eyes and take in a deep breath,
I feel myself melting into the mist.
It's cool but not uncomfortable.
It's like a touch of dew all over my skin.
I breathe out slowly and open my eyes, and there before me
They all stand or float; I can not see any feet.
They seem shy and withdrawn;
As though they are equally surprised to see me.
Such a wonder is this...they are real...
The people of the mist.

A Restless Night

It was just a whisper, but I'm sure I heard it right.
It was the flapping of wings, gently in the night.
At first it was overhead, maybe three feet away or so,
Then it whisked past my left side, so I turned to see it go.
My legs wouldn't move, I stood there so very still;
Even my breathing had stopped, I was frozen against my will.
I listened so intently, for any sound that I could hear,
But the silence it was deafening, as though nothing at all were near.
Within a split second I came to my senses; I bolted right out of there.
I ran and ran and ran so hard: whatever it was, I didn't care.
As I ran down the path before me, I kept listening from behind,
Was anything chasing me or was everything just in my mind?
Finally I came to a clearing; the moon was shining bright.
The darkness was left behind me, as I stepped into the light.
And there before me stood an angel of light, of enormous size.
The wings spread six feet at least and there was wisdom in those eyes.
I stumbled and I tripped, I wasn't sure what I should do.
The angel reached out a hand and helped me stand anew.
While never moving its' mouth, the angel conveyed to me,
I should never be afraid of things that I just can not see.
It wasn't really words it said, more like music to my ears.
The sound really hit a chord in me, it washed away my fears.
I wanted to ask the angel questions, but no sound, no words came out.
I couldn't even grunt or groan, I couldn't even shout.
Next thing I knew, I was awake in bed, having slept only a short time.
Whatever I had just dreamed about,
Was just as quickly leaving my mind.

She Stands Alone

She stands alone against the cold outside.

She is determined not to run and hide.

No matter what she must face from the coming storm;

Deep inside, her heart still burns warm.

And if no helpful soul comes around,

Have no fear, she will still stand her ground;

She'll face the fierce icy winds on her own,

Fighting the slashing rain that is thrown.

Life is harsh and storms abound,

Yet through all these tests, she has found...

The gentle breezes soon will bring

The warmth and new growth of the spring.

The sunshine will reach down and warm her face,

The tears from the harsh winter will leave no trace.

But this does not mean, no scars there'll be,

They have left their mark that you just can't see.

And when in the summer, the gentle breezes blow,

She can thrive in the warmth and take things slow.

For the fall is just around the corner

And more storms they will come,

But for now she is just grateful that the tempest is done.

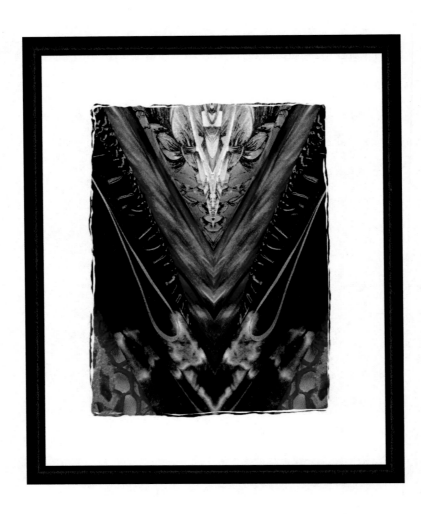

Bad Shirts

The first shirt I put on
Fits a little too tight.
The second shirt I tried
Just doesn't look right
The third shirt...well...
It'll just have to do.
But when this day is over
It's going in the trash too.
Sometimes I wonder
Whatever possessed me to buy?
Did an entity take over me
And say...go ahead...give it a try!
At the time it seemed fun
A statement I'll wear,
But the truth of it all
It just causes people to stare!
What was she thinking,
When she put that on today?
Did something possess her
To scare people away?
So with a smile on my face
Knowing this was just a quirk;
I guess I should be glad...
At least I made it to work!

We've All Been There

You never know when you open up to someone...
Will they actually be kind?
Or will they leave you feeling
That surely you must be blind!
Supposedly, if you never open up
You never can receive;
But how are you to know
If they are someone you can believe?
If you find yourself perplexed
By this very situation
You are probably questioning all they said
As just a clever manipulation.
Don't stress too much,
We've all been there...
It always hurts to find out
That someone doesn't care.
So what comes next?
Do you shut yourself down?
Hell no you don't!
Get rid of that frown!
Keep your heart and mind open
And continue to believe...
Because there really are souls out there
Who truly want to give and receive.

If I Could

If I could walk
Just a mile in your shoes
Where would they take me?
What direction would they choose?
If I could live your life
Just for a single day,
What insights would I gain
From living it your way?
If I could see through your eyes,
For a different point of view.
Would they be looking back at me
As I would be looking at you?
If I could seep into your brain,
Just for one single night;
Would your dreams be of happiness
Or would they be of fright?
If I could touch your soul
For a single moment in time...
Would it change your life forever
Or would it just change mine?

I Look In The Mirror

I look in the mirror,
Are those bags under my eyes?
Sigh, I'm getting older,
Most times I just don't realize.
In my mind I'm still young.
There are so many things I still want to do
But as my body is getting older,
The aches and pains...well I've had a few.
I walk and I hike,
I stay active every day
But some mornings I find,
It's hard to get out there and play.
Unbelievable to me, one half century
Has already passed me by.
Where did the time go?
Seems it was gone in the blink of an eye.
My deep dark hair now has streaks in it
Of such a lovely white.
People stop and ask if I've colored it this way?
You've got to be kidding, right?
I'm trying to grow old gracefully,
But no matter how hard I try
The winds of time overtake me
As I kiss my youth goodbye.

Holding Hands

Holding Hands...such a simple thing really.

It's a wonderful way of showing

"We are in this together".

Holding Hands...such a profound gesture.

It shows that together we will walk at the same pace.

With all of today's hustle and bustle

It shows that "we'll take whatever life throws at us,

With an equal stride".

Holding Hands...such a show of strength.

It lets each other know that by sharing the balance,

No one will trip or fall alone,

"We'll hold each other up whenever times get tough".

Holding Hands...such an intimate and silent way of saying

"I Love You".

The Joy Of Photography

Like a kid in a candy store,

That's what it is like for me

To take a lovely photo of a solitary tree.

And look over there, what is that I see?

A vibrant yellow flower with a busy little bee.

The more I look upon the ground

What is this that I have found?

A tiny little snail on a single blade of grass;

Oh, a photo of this would be first class.

The rocks, the stones, even tiny ant drones,

Everything has a beauty to me.

The broken fence, the rusty screw,

I love taking photos of these things too.

So if you happen to see me, with a camera in my hand

If I don't stop to chat, please do understand...

The more that I look, the more that I see,

Like a kid in a candy store and it's all for me!

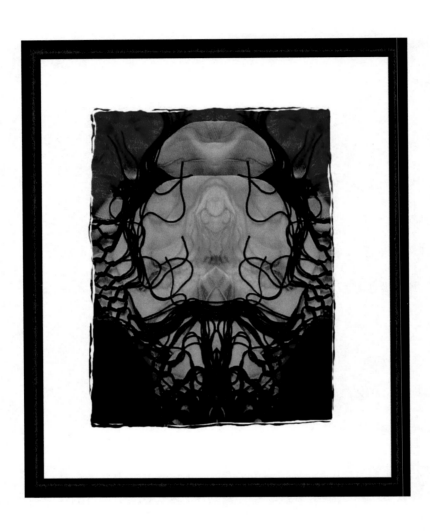

The Labyrinth Of My Mind

Go ahead; enter the tunnel into my mind,
I dare you to hide and seek and find.
The pathways are forever changing;
Leading to rooms I'm forever rearranging.
It's not that I want and hope you get lost,
It's just that letting you in comes at a cost.
Today my mind may light your way,
Tomorrow my mind may lead you astray.
Sometimes in darkness is when you can see my mind best
It has light and illumination;
It has waves of energy that crest.
My thoughts can send you spiraling into a void so deep
Or embrace and uplift you till your soul wants to weep.
I do not say these things just to scare you away,
I say these truths in the hopes that you'll stay;
At least for a little while so I can get used to you too
And then my mind will open up and actually let you through.
My mind is like a maze, a labyrinth if you will
If you enter with good intentions, all will be still.
If your own mind is open and your heart filled with song
I will share with you the wonders that I have known all along.
A mind is a repository, where all knowledge is stored
Past, present and future knowledge, here it is moored.
Some can only access the current, the here and the now
I can show you all the rest, this I can avow.
But be aware there is danger in accessing so much
The mind can play tricks at the slightest wrong touch.
You must be gentle when stroking the brain
You must take the utmost care not to cause any pain
Or the mind will shut down and spit you right out
This I can tell you without a single doubt.
So now you can see what challenges you will face,
If you choose to enter my mind and search around the place.
Enter here...

31546906R00035

Made in the USA
Middletown, DE
03 May 2016